Table of Contents

Introduction……………………………………....…2
Forward by Saul Roberts……………..…..…3
Pantry Items and Tools Needed………...4
Appetizers……………………………………..…5
Chicken………………….………………….……30
Beef……………………….………………….……73
Pork…………….……………………………….…90
Seafood……………………………………….…110
Sides……………………………………….……122
Index……...……………………………….……134

Introduction

For the last 10 years, I have been trying to perfect the recipe for lumpia and pancit noodles. After having it at multiple potlucks at work, I was determined to come up with the perfect recipe for both.

It wasn't until I met the love of my life, Saul whose favorite cuisine is Asian. He inspired me to try out different recipes and helped me critique each dish to make it perfectly balanced.

After that my love of cooking Asian food took off. Chow mein, fried rice, sushi... I couldn't stop experimenting with different styles of Asian cooking.

I hope you enjoy these recipes as much as we do and *cook with love*.

Sarah Jean Gilbert

Forward by Saul Roberts

We all know it's good to count our blessings. As a lifelong lover of Asian food, I feel like I need to hire a personal accountant to keep track of all the blessings I get being on the receiving end of the amazing dishes Sarah creates. If that weren't enough, being blessed with great cooking on my plate each night is not something new to me.

Growing up in my household, cooking was a one of the many ways my father artistically expressed himself. It was a nightly routine to see him in the kitchen after a long day at work.

My father loved to cook and I loved to eat so we made a great team. My fondest memories of my father's cooking was when he brought out his big Wok and made that rich, bold zing from his Szechuan sauce… that perfect marriage of texture and flavor of his stir fry… it was these dishes that I requested every year for my birthday. To me, it was pure love on a plate.

Reality set in after I left home and was left to fend for myself in the kitchen. It's amazing what we can take for granted until it's gone. I never again expected to be fortunate enough to have someone in my life cook for me that could hold a candle to my father's cooking. Those expectations came flying out the window the first time Sarah cooked for me. She somehow found a way to elevate all of my favorite Asian dishes in a way that I had never experienced. The bursting flavors in her creations dance on my tongue every time I take a bite.

I consider Sarah's culinary brilliance to be a blessing because like most people, my professional career, combined with life's challenges can bring with it a great deal of stress. Sarah's cooking is like a natural antidepressant for me, washing away all of my frustrations and worries the moment I bite into her blissful cuisine. By the time I'm halfway through my meal, I can hardly remember what I had been stressed about.

It's so exciting for me that Sarah is sharing her recipes with you. Her culinary antidotes for the common stresses of everyday life is just another way of her sharing her love of cooking with the rest of the world.

Pantry Items To Have On Hand

First thing you need to know is what to have in your pantry to cook most of these dishes in my book. I usually buy my ingredients from the local Asian store. Most chain stores will carry these ingredients.

Soy Sauce

Minced Garlic

Rice Vinegar

Oyster Sauce

Chinese 5 Spice Powder

Hoisin Sauce

Toasted Sesame Oil

Fish Sauce

Coconut Milk

Ginger Paste (found in the produce section; or use ground ginger in the spice section)

Lemongrass Paste (found in the produce section)

Sriracha Hot Sauce

Sambal Oelek (Garlic Chili Sauce)

Gochujang (Spicy Chili Paste)

Honey (good quality, makes the difference)

Cornstarch

Rice Flour (Mochiko flour)

Oil for frying (Peanut, canola, or vegetable)

Tools You Will Need

Cutting board, sharp knife

Wok, or large frying pan

Rice Cooker

Steam Basket

Blender or food processor

Egg Rolls

Ingredients

28 spring roll wrappers
4 cloves garlic, minced
8 oz ground pork
1 1/2 teaspoons ginger paste
1 teaspoon red pepper flakes
6 cups coleslaw mix
1/2 cup soy sauce
1 tablespoon rice wine vinegar
1/2 cup chopped green onion
1 tablespoon cornstarch
canola oil for cooking & frying

Directions

Heat enough oil in a large wok or nonstick pan to coat the bottom on medium high heat. Add pork, ginger, garlic and red pepper flakes to the wok/pan. Cook about 5-7 minutes, breaking up meat until it's coarse.

Whisk together soy sauce and cornstarch. Set aside.

Add coleslaw to the pan, stir to combine. Pour in soy sauce/cornstarch mixture. Cover and cook for 3-5 minutes or until sauce has thickened. Once thickened, turn off the heat and allow mixture to cool completely.

Heat 1/4 inch oil in a large, deep skillet until temperature reaches 375 degrees.

Spoon tablespoon size amounts of mixture across (just below) center of spring roll wrapper. Fold bottom point of wrapper up over the filling; fold side points over next, forming an envelope shape. Roll tightly. Set aside. Repeat until all mixture has been used.

Fry in batches 2-4 minutes on each side or until golden and crispy. Remove with a slotted spoon, draining on a paper towel lined baking sheet.

Serve immediately with sweet and sour sauce.

Serves 6-8

Lumpia

The Filipino version of egg rolls with a crispier, thinner wrapper and light filling.

Ingredients

1 tablespoon vegetable oil
1 medium sweet onion, diced
4 cloves garlic, minced
1 cup shredded carrots
1 tablespoon ginger paste
1 lb ground pork
1 teaspoon salt
1 1/2 teaspoons pepper
1 tablespoon soy sauce
1/4 cup green onion, minced
4 tablespoons cilantro, minced
2 cups canola oil for frying
25-30 lumpia wrappers
1 egg, beaten
Sweet chili sauce, for serving

Directions

Heat oil in a medium pan over medium high heat. Add onion, garlic, ginger and carrot. Cook 5-7 minutes, stirring constantly. Add ground pork and use a meat masher to break up pork until it is a fine consistency. Cook for 7 minutes. Add salt, pepper and soy sauce. Stir well. Add cilantro and green onion. Remove pan from heat and allow to cool.

Heat oil in a deep frying pan or cast iron skillet until it reaches 300 degrees.

Lay out one lumpia wrapper in a diamond shape. Add 2 tablespoons of filling at the bottom of the wrapper, brush the top/tip of the "diamond" with egg wash and roll tightly from the filling side up, folding the sides in like a burrito. Repeat until you are out of filling. Fry 4 to 6 lumpia at a time in the skillet, draining on a plate lined with a paper towel.

Serve hot with sweet chili sauce.

Serves 10.

Tip: If you are making A LOT of lumpia, it is best to heat the oven to 325 degrees and place finished lumpia in a large roasting pan after draining on paper towels. This will keep them warm until ready to serve.

Pot Stickers

A traditional pot sticker filled with ground pork, or ground chicken.

Ingredients

36 wonton/pot sticker wrappers

oil for frying

1 large egg, beaten

Filling

1 lb ground pork or ground chicken

3/4 cup coleslaw mix

2 oz diced shitake mushrooms

2 tablespoons hoisin sauce

1 1/2 tablespoons ginger paste

2 teaspoons sesame oil

2 teaspoons sriracha hot sauce

1 teaspoon ground black pepper

2 tablespoons chives (fresh or dried)

2 cloves of garlic, minced

Directions

Mix all filling ingredients in a large bowl with a wooden spoon and stir to combine. Add 1/2-1 tablespoon filling (depending on the size of your wonton wrappers) in the middle of each wrapper, brush lightly with egg wash to seal and fold.

As you are folding the pot stickers, heat oil on medium in a large skillet or wok, adding enough oil to cover bottom of the pan. Fry pot stickers for 3 minutes on each side. Preheat oven to 300 degrees and place cooked pot stickers on a cookie sheet to keep warm until you are ready to serve.

Serve hot with dipping sauce.

Serves 9

Pot Sticker Sauce

Ingredients

1/4 cup + 2 tablespoons soy sauce

1/4 cup rice vinegar

1 teaspoon korean chili flakes

1 tablespoon light brown sugar

1 tablespoon chives, dried

2 cloves garlic, minced

2 teaspoons ginger paste

1 teaspoon sesame oil

Directions:

Mix all ingredients together in a small bowl and refrigerate at least 2 hours.

Cream Cheese Rangoon (Traditional or Crab)

Ingredients

Filling
8 oz cream cheese, room temperature
2 tablespoons scallions, minced
1/2 tablespoon minced garlic
dash Worcestershire sauce
6 oz crab meat (optional)

Wontons
24 wonton wrappers
1 egg, beaten (egg wash)
oil for frying

Directions

Pour oil into a large pan and heat to 350 degrees. In a medium bowl, combine all filling ingredients, beat with a hand mixer until light and fluffy.

Spoon mixture into the middle of each wonton and fold up the sides, sealing with egg wash. Fry in hot oil until golden brown, drain on paper towels and cool for 10 minutes before serving.

Serves 6.

BBQ Pork

Ingredients

24 oz pork tenderloin

Marinade

1/4 cup soy sauce

2 tablespoons dry red wine

1 tablespoon brown sugar

1 tablespoon honey

2 teaspoons red food coloring

1/4 teaspoon cinnamon

2 garlic cloves, minced

Directions

Whisk together all marinade ingredients in a medium bowl and set aside. Place pork in a large pan or zip lock bag and cover with marinade. Refrigerate overnight.

Preheat oven to 350 degrees. Place pork on a roasting rack and bake 45 minutes, basting every 10 minutes with marinade. Let meat rest 15-20 minutes before slicing. Serve with hot mustard for dipping.

Serves 8.

Chicken Lettuce Wraps

Ingredients

2 tablespoons sesame oil, divided
1 cup mushrooms, chopped
1 lb. ground chicken
2 garlic cloves, minced
6 basil leaves, finely chopped
2 tablespoons hoisin sauce
2 tablespoons teriyaki sauce
1 tablespoon soy sauce
1 tablespoon rice wine vinegar

Directions

In a medium wok or skillet on medium heat, add 1 tablespoon of sesame oil. Add mushrooms, cook, stirring occasionally until golden brown and softened (about 5 minutes); transfer to a plate and set aside.

Add remaining sesame oil to the skillet and turn the heat up to medium high. Add ground chicken and cook until done, about 4-5 minutes, crumbling the meat as it cooks. Drain fat, if needed. Add minced garlic and stir for 30 seconds. Add mushrooms then sprinkle in basil leaves; stir to combine.

In a small bowl, combine hoisin sauce, teriyaki sauce, soy sauce, rice wine vinegar, ground ginger, cornstarch and sriracha. Whisk to combine. Pour sauce over chicken mixture and stir to coat evenly. Cook until heated through and slightly thickened, about 3-5 minutes. Serve with lettuce "cups."

Serves 4.

Thai Lettuce Wraps

Thai Chicken Satays

Ingredients

1 lb boneless, skinless chicken breast
1/4 cup soy sauce
2 tablespoons fresh lime juice
2 cloves garlic, minced
1 teaspoon grated fresh ginger
3/4 teaspoon red pepper flakes
2 tablespoons water
4 green onions, cut into 1 inch pieces
8 Bamboo skewers (10-12 inches long)

Directions

Cut chicken into 3/4 inch strips, place in a shallow glass dish and set aside.

Combine soy sauce, lime juice, garlic, ginger and red pepper flakes in a small bowl. Add water and mix thoroughly. Pour over chicken and toss to coat evenly. Cover and marinate in the refrigerator for at least 30 minutes, up to 2 hours, stirring occasionally.

Soak bamboo skewers 20 minutes in cold water to keep them from burning. Drain the chicken and reserve the marinade. Weave the chicken strips onto each skewer, alternating with green onion pieces. You may need to use several pieces to cover each skewer.

Brush chicken and onions with reserved marinade. Place skewers on a grill and cook over medium heat.

Thai Coconut Curry Noodles

Ingredients

12 oz fresh egg noodles
1 tablespoon minced garlic cloves
1 tablespoon red curry paste
1 cup coconut milk
1 cup chicken broth
1 tablespoon curry powder
1 pinch turmeric powder
1 tablespoon fish sauce
1 tablespoon lime juice

Directions

Heat a large saucepan on high heat filled 3/4 of the way with water until boiling. Turn off heat. Add noodles, separating with a fork. Let the noodles soak until tender or according to the directions on the package. Drain and keep warm.

In a medium saucepan, heat coconut milk on low heat and slowly stir in the curry paste. When it begins to simmer, add in the remaining ingredients. Continue to simmer for approximately 2 minutes. Stir in the noodles and serve.

Thai Marinated Cucumbers

Ingredients

1/3 cup rice vinegar
1/4 cup sugar
1/4 cup water
1/4 teaspoon salt
1/4 teaspoon ground black pepper
1 large cucumber, seeded

Directions

Combine vinegar, sugar, water and salt in a small saucepan and cook over medium heat, stirring until it boils and the sugar is dissolved. Remove from heat and let it cool to room temperature.

Peel the cucumber and cut lengthwise into quarters and again crosswise into 1/8 slices. Place in a serving bowl and pour marinade over cucumbers, stirring to blend. Cover and refrigerate for 2 hours or overnight.

Tamarind Cashew Dipping Sauce

Ingredients

1/4 cup chopped cashews
1 tablespoon hoisin sauce
2 medium garlic cloves, minced
2 green onions, chopped
1/2 teaspoon ground black pepper
1/4 teaspoon cayenne pepper
1/4 cup canola oil
3 teaspoons honey
6 tablespoons rice wine vinegar
1/2 teaspoon tamarind pulp
1/2 teaspoon toasted sesame seeds

Directions

Combine cashews, hoisin sauce, garlic, green onion, cayenne pepper and black pepper in a blender or food processor and puree until smooth.

In a small saucepan add oil, honey, rice wine vinegar and tamarind pulp. Heat at medium for 1 minute. Stir until the tamarind pulp is completely dissolved. Add to cashew mixture and blend until smooth. Pour into small serving bowl and sprinkle with toasted sesame seeds. Refrigerate for at least 30 minutes.

Peanut Sauce

Ingredients

1/4 cup creamy peanut butter
2 tablespoons water
4 tablespoons sugar
1 tablespoon soy sauce
1 teaspoon rice vinegar
1 teaspoon lime juice
1/2 teaspoon chili oil

Directions

Combine peanut butter, water, sugar, soy sauce, rice vinegar, lime juice and chili oil in a small saucepan. Whisk over medium heat until it begins to bubble. Cover the pan and remove from heat. Allow to cool to room temperature before serving.

Sweet Chili Dipping Sauce

Ingredients

1/4 cup rice wine vinegar
2 tablespoons fish sauce
1/4 cup hot water
2 tablespoons sugar
1 lime, juiced
1 teaspoon garlic, minced
1 teaspoon red chili paste

Directions

Combine all ingredients in a blender and puree until smooth. Serve.

Serves 4.

Salad Rolls

Ingredients

10-12 large shrimp, deveined

1 cucumber julienned (3-4" long)

2-3 small carrots julienned (3-4" long)

4 oz rice noodles

leaves from 1 small head romaine lettuce, spine removed

1 cup cilantro

1/2 cup fresh mint leaves

1 teaspoon canola oil

1 teaspoon soy sauce

10 rice paper wraps

salt

peanut dipping sauce (recipe page 19)

Directions

Heat oil in a medium skillet on medium heat. Add shrimp, 1 teaspoon soy sauce and salt, if necessary. Sauté the shrimp for about 2-3 minutes or until cooked all the way through. Let it cool for about 5 minutes.

Meanwhile, cook noodles according to package instructions. Once cooked, drain and rinse with cold water to stop the cooking process. Set aside.

Cut cooked shrimp in half lengthwise. Pour warm water in a large skillet or pie plate. Dip rice paper wrap in warm water for 10-15 seconds and then spread it carefully on a slightly wet cutting board, laying it flat.

Start to layer your salad rolls. Start with lettuce, next the noodles, 3 shrimp, 2-3 carrot juliennes, 2-3 cucumber juliennes, cilantro and finally 3-4 mint leaves on one side of the wet wrap. Gently fold the rice paper (like a burrito), making sure to roll it tightly so fillings do not come out.

Serve with peanut dipping sauce.

Serves 4.

Crispy Green Beans

Ingredients

4 egg whites

3 cups flour

2 3/4 cups club soda

about 6 cups canola oil, for frying

1 lb green beans, trimmed

sea salt

Directions

In a large bowl with a hand mixer, beat egg whites until soft peaks form. Whisk in flour and club soda. Place the batter in the refrigerator until ready to use.

Pour oil into a large pot or dutch oven so that it is at least a few inches deep. Heat to 350 degrees over medium-high. Dip the trimmed beans into the batter, letting the excess run off. Carefully lower them into the hot oil in small batches, so that they do not stick together. Fry until the batter is golden brown and the beans are bright green, about 3 minutes. Remove with a slotted spoon and place on a paper towel-lined plate. Season with salt. Repeat until the beans are finished. Serve with spicy dipping sauce.

Serves 4.

Spicy Sauce for Green Beans

Ingredients

1 cup Japanese Mayonnaise (Kewpie brand is best)
2 1/2 tablespoons hot chili sauce (sriracha)
6 green onions, whites only, coarsely chopped
4 garlic cloves, coarsely chopped
1/2 teaspoon prepared horseradish

Directions

Add all ingredients to a medium size bowl and whisk well to combine.

Refrigerate at least 4 hours or overnight.

Chinese Pork Meatballs

Ingredients

1 lb ground pork
1 tablespoon cornstarch
1 teaspoon minced ginger
3 garlic cloves, minced
2 teaspoons brown sugar
2 teaspoons soy sauce
1 teaspoon Five-Spice powder
2 pinches ground white pepper
3 tablespoons peanut oil

Sauce

3 tablespoons soy sauce
3 tablespoons sweet soy sauce
3 tablespoons fish sauce
1 teaspoon rice vinegar
2-3 tablespoons sriracha sauce
green onions or chives for garnish

Directions

In a large bowl, combine pork, cornstarch, ginger, garlic, brown sugar, soy sauce, Five-Spice powder and pepper, mix well.

Roll 1 heaping tablespoon of pork mixture into a ball and continue until all the pork mixture is used (about 20 small meatballs).

In a wok or large skillet over medium heat, heat peanut oil. Using a spatula, spread the oil to coat enough of the surface to fry about 10 meatballs at a time. Lower the meatballs into the wok (or frying pan) in batches.

Cook 2 minutes, or until the bottoms are lightly browned. Use the spatula to carefully rotate the meatballs to cook on the other sides. Brown all sides. Keep rotating the meatballs gently until cooked through, about 7-10 minutes.

Sauce

Combine all ingredients except garnish and stir to mix well. Sriracha sauce can be adjusted according to taste. Dice green onion. Serve sauce in dipping bowls on the side and drizzle lightly over the top of meatballs. Sprinkle additional green onion over the top for presentation.

Serves 4.

Easy Sweet & Sour Meatballs

Ingredients

1 5 lb bag of frozen meatballs, store bought
1 33 oz container sweet chili sauce
1 15 oz can pineapple chunks (with juice)
1 large sweet onion, quartered
1 large white onion, quartered

Directions

Add all ingredients to a large crock pot and cook 8-10 hours on low heat or 4 hours on high heat until meatballs are hot and onion is tender.

Serve hot over rice.

Serves 8-10.

Korean Meatballs

Ingredients

1/2 lb ground chicken
1/2 lb ground beef
1/2 cup bread crumbs
1/2 cup parmesan cheese
1 egg
1/2 teaspoon salt
1/2 teaspoon white pepper
1/4 cup fresh cilantro
1 clove garlic, minced
1 tablespoon ginger paste
1/4 medium sized sweet onion, diced
1/2 teaspoon sesame oil
1 teaspoon low sodium soy sauce
freshly ground black pepper

Directions

Add all ingredients in a large mixing bowl. Stir with a large wooden spoon until well mixed.

Form 1 inch meatballs and place on a parchment lined, brimmed baking sheet.

Bake at 350 degrees for 40 minutes or fry in batches in dutch oven with 2 inches of oil. Cook about 3-5 minutes on each side until completely browned, draining on paper towel-lined baking sheet or plate.

Makes 30 meatballs.

Rumaki

Ingredients

1/4 lb chicken livers

1/4 cup soy sauce

1 tablespoon ginger paste

2 tablespoons brown sugar

1 teaspoon curry powder

12 water chestnuts (from the can, rinsed, drained and cut in half)

8 thick cut bacon slices, cut into thirds

24 wooden toothpicks soaked in cold water for 1 hour

Directions

Cut chicken livers into 24 (roughly 1/2-inch) pieces. Stir together soy sauce, ginger, brown sugar and curry powder in a small bowl. Add livers and water chestnuts and toss to coat. Refrigerate for 1 hour.

Preheat broiler. Remove livers and chestnuts from marinade; discard marinade. Place a piece of bacon on a work surface and place liver and a chestnut half in center. Wrap bacon around liver and chestnut and secure with a wooden pick. Continue until all livers and chestnuts are used.

Broil rumaki on rack of broiler pan 2 inches from heat, turning once, until bacon is crisp and livers are cooked but still slightly pink inside (unwrap one to check for doneness), 5 to 6 minutes. Serve immediately.

Serves 6.

Chinese Chicken Batter 1

A very fluffy batter, crisp on the outside and fluffy on the inside.

Ingredients

1 cup flour

1 1/2 teaspoons baking powder

pinch of salt

1 egg, beaten

2/3 cup milk

2 lbs boneless, skinless chicken, cut into bite size pieces

Directions

Mix together all dry ingredients. Add egg and milk. Mix well. Dip chicken pieces in the batter to coat.

Heat a large skillet on medium heat with enough canola oil (canola is my preferred, use what you have on hand) to fry (about 2 inches). Heat oil to 325 degrees.

Fry until browned on both sides and chicken has "puffed."

Serves 4.

Chinese Chicken Batter 2

A crispier chicken batter that holds up well with heavy sauces.

Ingredients

4 large egg whites

3/4 cup cornstarch

1/3 cup water

1 lb chicken breast, cut into 1 inch bite size pieces

oil for frying

Directions

In a large bowl, add egg whites and whisk until foamy, about 3-5 minutes. Add in cornstarch and water. Whisk until combined. Gently fold in chicken.

Heat a large skillet on medium heat with enough canola oil (canola is my preferred, use what you have on hand) to fry (about 2 inches). Heat oil to 325 degrees.

Cook chicken 2-3 minutes on each side, turning once. Drain on paper towels. Serve with sauce of choice.

Serves 4.

SAUCES FOR CHICKEN

Orange Sauce

Ingredients

1 1/2 cups water

1/4 cup orange juice

1/3 cup rice vinegar

2 1/2 tablespoons soy sauce

1 tablespoon orange zest, finely grated

1 cup packed brown sugar

1 teaspoon grated ginger or ginger paste

1 teaspoon garlic, minced

2 tablespoons green onion, chopped

1 teaspoon red pepper flakes

Cornstarch Slurry

3 tablespoons cornstarch

2 tablespoons water

Directions

In a large saucepan combine water, orange juice, vinegar and soy sauce. Stir well over medium high heat for a few minutes. Stir in remaining ingredients and bring to a boil.

In a small bowl, whisk together cornstarch and water to make a slurry. When the sauce mixture comes to a boil, reduce to a simmer and slowly add slurry, whisking until it thickens.

Serve hot over chicken.

Honey Sesame Sauce

Ingredients

2 tablespoons honey

2 tablespoons sweet chili sauce

6 tablespoons ketchup

4 tablespoons soy sauce

1/2 cup water

Toasted sesame seeds to top

Directions

In a medium saucepan, combine all sauce ingredients except sesame seeds. Heat on medium high until sauce comes to a boil and sauce has thickened. Pour over chicken and toss with sesame seeds to serve.

Sweet and Sour Sauce

Ingredients

1 cup canned pineapple juice

3/4 cup packed light brown sugar

1/3 cup rice vinegar

3 tablespoons ketchup

2 tablespoons soy sauce

2 drops red food coloring (optional)

Cornstarch slurry

1 tablespoon cornstarch dissolved into 1 1/2 tablespoons water

Directions

Place all ingredients, except for the slurry and food coloring in a small saucepan and bring to a boil. Reduce heat to simmer and slowly add slurry mixture. If using red food coloring, stir it in and whisk until well combined. Serve hot over chicken or with spring rolls for dipping.

Lemon Sauce

Ingredients

1 cup water

2 tablespoons lemon juice

1 tablespoon lemon zest, grated

1/2 cup sugar

2 drops yellow food coloring

Cornstarch slurry

1 tablespoon cornstarch dissolved into 1 1/2 tablespoons water.

Directions

Combine all ingredients, except slurry, in a small saucepan over medium high heat. Bring to a boil. Reduce heat to low and slowly stir in slurry mixture. Add food coloring and whisk until well combined.

General Tso's Sauce

Ingredients

1 tablespoon vegetable or canola oil

2 cloves garlic, minced

1 teaspoon ginger paste

1/2 cup dried chili pods

1/4 cup rice wine

1/4 cup soy sauce

1/4 cup rice wine vinegar

1/4 cup sugar

Cornstarch slurry

1 tablespoon cornstarch dissolved into 1 1/2 tablespoons water.

Directions

In a large skillet or wok, heat oil on low-medium heat. Add garlic and ginger, stirring frequently for 3 minutes. Add dried chili pods and stir well for one minute then add remaining sauce ingredients. Turn heat up to medium high and bring mixture to a boil. Reduce heat to simmer. Whisk in slurry mixture. Toss with chicken.

Honey Walnut Sauce

Ingredients

1/4 cup honey
1/2 cup mayonnaise
4 tablespoons sweetened condensed milk
1/2 cup toasted whole walnuts

Directions

In a large bowl, whisk together mayonnaise, honey and sweetened condensed milk.

Toast nuts in the oven at 350 degrees for 10 minutes. Cool slightly and add to sauce, toss with cooked (battered) chicken (Chicken Batter 2, page 32).

Cashew Chicken

Ingredients

3 large boneless, skinless chicken breasts

1/2 large white onion, sliced

1 cup diced celery

1 cup cashews

1 teaspoon red chili pepper flakes

Green onion and sesame seeds for garnish

Sauce

1/2 cup soy sauce

1/4 cup vegetable broth

1/4 cup brown sugar

2 cloves minced garlic

1 tablespoon ginger paste

1 teaspoon sesame oil

2 teaspoons cornstarch

Directions

Heat wok or large pan over medium high heat with vegetable oil or canola oil.

Season chicken lightly with salt, pepper and chili flakes. Add chicken to hot wok/pan and cook about 7-10 minutes. Remove chicken, place on a plate and set aside. Add vegetables to the pan. Saute 5-7 minutes or until tender.

Add all sauce ingredients to a blender and blend until well combined. Add chicken back into the pan with vegetables and pour in sauce. Stir to combine. Simmer on low heat until sauce has thickened.

Add cashews, stir to combine. Serve topped with sesame seeds and green onion.

Serves 4.

Bourbon Chicken

Ingredients

2 lbs boneless, skinless chicken breasts, cut into bite size pieces
1 tablespoon oil
2 garlic cloves, minced
1 teaspoon ginger paste
1 teaspoon crushed chili flakes
1/4 cup apple juice
1/3 cup light brown sugar
2 tablespoons ketchup
1 tablespoon cider vinegar
1/2 cup water
1/3 cup soy sauce
1 1/2 tablespoons cornstarch

Directions

Heat oil in a large skillet. Add chicken and cook until lightly browned. Remove chicken and set aside. Dissolve cornstarch in cold water or soy sauce, whisk until well combined. In a small saucepan add all sauce ingredients except slurry and heat to a boil. Slowly add in slurry mixture. Reduce heat to low. Add to chicken and serve over hot rice.

Serves 4.

Szechuan Chicken

Ingredients

1 teaspoon sugar

4 cloves garlic, minced

1 tablespoon vegetable oil

1 1/2 tablespoons white wine vinegar

3 tablespoons cornstarch

5 tablespoons low-sodium soy sauce

1/8 teaspoon cayenne pepper, or to taste

1/4 cup water

4 boneless, skinless chicken breasts, cut into cubes

3 green onions, sliced diagonally into 1/2 inch pieces

Directions

In a Ziploc bag or large bowl, add cornstarch and chicken. Toss to coat.

Over medium-high heat, heat oil in a large skillet. Fry garlic and chicken pieces until lightly browned, stirring constantly.

Whisk together vinegar, sugar, soy sauce, cayenne pepper and water in a small bowl. Pour in the skillet with chicken and garlic. Cover and cook 3 to 5 minutes until chicken is cooked all the way through.

Stir in green onion and cook for 2 minutes uncovered. Serve over steamed rice.

Serves 4.

Grilled Sweet Chili Chicken

Ingredients

1 lb boneless, skinless chicken thighs

Marinade

1 tablespoon chives
1 cup sweet chili sauce
1/4 cup soy sauce
2 tablespoons lemon juice
2 tablespoons oil
salt and pepper, to taste

Directions

Add marinade ingredients into a large Ziploc bag and shake to mix. Add chicken and toss to coat evenly. Marinate overnight.

The next day, heat your grill and spray evenly with nonstick cooking spray. Grill chicken on both sides until cooked all the way through, about 6-7 minutes per side.

Serve hot with sticky rice and pasta salad or steamed vegetables.

Serves 4.

Peking Chicken

Ingredients

1 whole chicken, cut into sections

1/2 teaspoon Five-Spice powder

Marinade

1/4 cup light soy sauce

2 tablespoons dark soy sauce

1 tablespoon sugar

2 tablespoons ginger paste

1 teaspoon Five-Spice powder

Basting Sauce

Leftover marinade (cooked)

2 tablespoons honey

Directions

Rub the inside of the chicken with Five-Spice powder. In a large bowl or Ziploc bag, combine the marinade. Add chicken pieces to the bag. Marinate for a minimum of 4 hours (preferably overnight) in the refrigerator.

Remove chicken from the refrigerator 30 minutes prior to cooking. Set up a baking sheet with a rack and set chicken pieces on top.

Add leftover marinade to a small saucepan. Cook 5-10 minutes on low heat. Add 2 tablespoons of honey at the end to sweeten and thicken. Set marinade aside for basting at the end.

Preheat oven to 350 degrees. Bake chicken for 20 minutes. After 20 minutes, you should see oil drippings. Baste chicken with the oil every 20 minutes for an hour. (If you don't get any oil drippings, you can use 1-2 tablespoons of oil and brush it on instead).

After chicken has cooked for 1 hour, start basting it with the basting sauce every 10-15 minutes or until the marinade is used up (approximately 30 minutes).

Remove chicken when the temperature reaches 165 degrees. Depending on the size of the chicken, cooking times will vary.

Allow chicken to rest 10-15 minutes before slicing.

Serves 4-6.

Caramelized Lemongrass Chicken

Ingredients

4 tablespoons lemongrass paste

2 lbs boneless, skinless chicken thighs

2 1/2 tablespoons fish sauce

1/4 cup sugar

2 cloves garlic, minced

1/2 teaspoon black pepper

1 tablespoon vegetable or canola oil

1 tablespoon lime juice

Directions

In a large Ziploc bag or mixing bowl, add lemongrass paste, fish sauce, sugar, garlic, pepper and lime juice. Add chicken to the marinade and allow to marinate overnight for best flavor.

Heat oil in a large skillet or wok on medium heat. Remove chicken from bag, reserve marinade. Cook chicken 10-15 minutes or until browned, turning only once. Pour reserved marinade in the skillet and bring to a boil. Reduce heat to low, cover and simmer 20-30 minutes or until chicken is cooked all the way through, turning chicken occasionally.

Serves 4.

Thai Grilled Chicken

Ingredients

12 boneless, skinless chicken thighs

Marinade

1/3 cup chopped fresh basil
1/3 cup chopped cilantro
1 tablespoon minced ginger, or paste
1 tablespoon minced garlic
1 tablespoon minced chili pepper
1 1/2 tablespoons soy sauce
1 1/2 tablespoons fish sauce
1 1/2 tablespoons olive oil
1 1/2 tablespoons brown sugar

Directions

Combine all marinade ingredients in a large bowl. Whisk well. Add chicken and allow to marinate at least 1 hour or preferably overnight for best flavor.

Grill chicken on the BBQ until cooked all the way through, about 7 minutes each side.

Serves 4.

Honey Sriracha Chicken

Ingredients

4 bone-in chicken thighs

3 cloves garlic, minced

1 tablespoon oil

1 tablespoon toasted sesame seeds

Marinade

1 1/2 tablespoons honey

1 tablespoon soy sauce

1/2 tablespoon sriracha chili sauce

1 teaspoon rice vinegar

pinch of salt and pepper

Directions

Whisk marinade together in a large bowl. Reserve half. Marinate the chicken in the remaining marinade and refrigerate overnight or at least 2 hours.

Heat oven to 400 degrees. Remove chicken from marinade and place on a lined baking sheet (with parchment or foil) and bake 20-30 minutes or until chicken is slightly charred; brushing with extra marinade every 10 minutes.

Serves 4.

Korean Fried Chicken

Ingredients

2 lbs boneless, skinless chicken thighs, cut into 1 inch pieces

1/4 cup flour

2 eggs

1/2 cup cornstarch

oil for frying

Sauce

1/3 cup gochugang red pepper paste

3 tablespoons rice vinegar

1/4 cup brown sugar

2 tablespoons soy sauce

1 tablespoon toasted sesame seeds, for garnish

Directions

Toss chicken in flour, then dredge in egg and coat in cornstarch.

In a large glass bowl, add the sauce ingredients together (except sesame seeds), whisking well.

Heat a heavy bottomed pan with 3 inches of oil to 375 degrees. Fry the chicken 3-4 minutes or until browned and crispy. Drain the chicken and add to the sauce. Toss to combine and garnish with sesame seeds.

Serves 4.

Thai Green Curry

Ingredients

Curry

4-6 tablespoons Thai green curry paste
2 large garlic cloves, *minced*
2 teaspoons fresh ginger, *finely grated*
1 tablespoon lemongrass paste

Sauce

2 tablespoons vegetable oil
1 cup chicken broth
14 oz coconut milk
1-3 teaspoons fish sauce
1-3 teaspoons sugar
1/8 teaspoon salt
6 lime leaves
6 medium sized boneless, skinless chicken thighs
1 1/2 cups snow peas
16 Thai basil leaves
Juice of 1/2 lime

Garnishes

Crispy fried Asian shallots
Thai basil or cilantro
Green or red chilies slices

Directions

Cook chicken in oven, on the grill (highly recommended) or in a large skillet/wok until cooked all the way through. Cut into bite size pieces and set aside.

Heat oil in a large skillet or dutch oven over medium high heat. Add curry paste, garlic, ginger and lemongrass paste. Cook 3-5 minutes or until it has a "dry" appearance. Whisk in chicken broth, coconut milk, sugar, fish sauce and salt. Add snow peas, cook 3-5 minutes or until slightly softened, then stir in basil and lime juice. Turn off heat and add cooked chicken thighs, stir well to combine.

Serve hot over jasmine rice and garnish.

Serves 4.

Thai Red Curry

Ingredients

1 tablespoon cooking oil
5 boneless, skinless chicken thighs
2 tablespoons red Thai curry paste
2 cloves garlic, minced
1 tablespoon ginger paste
13 oz can coconut milk
1 cup chicken broth
1/4 teaspoon fish sauce
5 cups cooked jasmine or basmati rice
1/4 cup cilantro
2-3 green onions
1 lime

Directions

Heat a large, deep skillet or saucepan over medium heat. Add cooking oil, then swirl to cover the surface of the skillet. Add chicken thighs and cook until browned on each side (about 3-5 minutes each side). Remove chicken from the skillet.

Add Thai curry paste, minced garlic and grated ginger to the skillet. Stir and saute the aromatics for one minute. Add coconut milk, chicken broth and fish sauce to the skillet. Stir to combine and dissolve any browned bits off the bottom of the skillet. Add the chicken back to the skillet, cover and allow to simmer. Turn the heat down to low or medium-low and let the thighs simmer in the coconut sauce for 15 minutes.

To serve, scoop 1 cup of cooked rice into the bottom of each bowl. Add one of the braised chicken thighs, then top with a ladle or two of the coconut broth. Add fresh cilantro leaves, sliced green onion and a wedge or two of fresh lime to each bowl.

Serves 4

Thai Yellow Curry

Ingredients

1 tablespoon vegetable oil
4 tablespoons yellow curry paste
2 15-ounce cans of coconut milk
2 cups chicken stock
4 carrots, peeled and sliced into 1/8" rounds
4 medium-size potatoes, peeled and cut into bite-size pieces
1 yellow onion, sliced into wedges, then halved
1 can baby corn, drained
2 chicken breasts, very thinly sliced
1 1/2 teaspoons fish sauce
3/4 teaspoon salt
1 1/2 teaspoons sugar
cilantro, for garnish
serve with jasmine rice

Directions

Bring a pot of salted water to a boil on high heat, boil potatoes until fork-tender. Drain and set aside.

In a large pot, heat oil on medium low. Add curry paste to oil, stir 3-5 minutes. Stir in coconut milk and chicken stock, bring to a boil. Add carrots, corn and onions.

Once carrots are almost fork-tender, add sliced chicken and cook 5 minutes. Remove from heat. Stir in potatoes, fish sauce, salt and sugar. Cook 5-7 minutes on medium heat.

Turn off the heat and serve over rice, garnish with fresh cilantro.

Serves 4

Evil Jungle Princess (Thai Curry)

Ingredients

1 can baby corn, drained and cut into thirds

1 tablespoon red curry paste

2 tablespoons lemongrass paste

2-3 lime leaves (or 1 tablespoon lime juice)

2 tablespoons brown sugar

1 tablespoon peanut butter

2 tablespoons garlic chili sauce

13 oz coconut milk, unsweetened

chicken breasts cut into 1/4 inch strips, or beef cut into strips

1/2 cup red bell pepper, cut into 1/4 inch strips

1 teaspoon lime juice

1/4 cup fresh Thai basil, chopped, or regular basil

1/4 cup fresh mint leaves, chopped

roasted peanuts, crushed

Jasmine rice

Directions

Cook rice on the stove top or rice cooker while preparing your dish.

Combine coconut milk, red curry paste, lemon grass paste, lime leaves (or additional juice), fish sauce, sugar, peanut butter and garlic chili sauce in a large saute pan. Bring to a simmer.

Add chicken and bell pepper strips. Cook until chicken is done and curry sauce is thick enough to coat the back of a spoon. Add lime juice and fresh herbs. Stir until well combined.

Serve hot over jasmine rice and top with peanuts.

Serves 4.

Chicken Pad Thai

Ingredients

10 oz Thai rice noodles

1 lb boneless, skinless chicken breasts, cut into small strips

2 tablespoons vegetable oil (or canola oil)

1/4 cup packed, dark brown sugar

1/4 cup soy sauce

2 tablespoons rice vinegar

1 1/2 tablespoons lime juice

1 tablespoon fish sauce

1/2 red bell pepper, sliced into strips

1/2 green bell pepper, sliced into strips

2 cups matchstick carrots

4 cloves garlic, minced

4 green onions, minced

2 cups bean sprouts

3 large eggs

1/2 cup unsalted peanuts, roughly chopped

1/2 cup cilantro, chopped

Directions

Prepare rice noodles according to directions on package. Drain and set aside.

In a medium sized mixing bowl, combine brown sugar, soy sauce, vinegar, lime juice and fish sauce. Set aside.

Heat oil in a wok or large skillet over medium high heat. Add chicken and saute until cooked through, about 4-6 minutes. Transfer to a plate, leaving the oil remaining in the pan.

Add peppers and carrots. Saute about 3 minutes. Add garlic, green onion and bean sprouts. Saute additional 2-3 minutes. Push vegetables to the side of the pan and crack eggs in the center. Cook and scramble until eggs are cooked all the way through.

Add chicken, noodles and sauce. Toss everything together and cook an additional 2-3 minutes. Serve warm topped with cilantro, peanuts, red pepper flakes and sesame seeds.

Serves 4.

Chicken Pad Thai 2

Ingredients

Sauce

3/4 cup chicken stock

2 tablespoons soy sauce

2 tablespoons fish sauce

6 tablespoons light brown sugar

3 tablespoons creamy peanut butter

2 tablespoons lime juice

2 tablespoons rice wine vinegar

2 tablespoons sriracha

1/2 tablespoon ginger paste

1 tablespoon minced garlic

Pad Thai

4 oz rice noodles

1 teaspoon canola oil

1 large egg, beaten

2 large chicken breasts, cubed

1/2 cup bean sprouts

For the garnish

Chopped cilantro

Chopped peanuts

Lime wedges

Directions

Whisk together sauce ingredients and set aside.

Cook noodles according to directions. Drain and set aside.

Preheat a skillet or wok on medium heat and add oil. Cook chicken until mostly done. Push chicken over to the side of the pan and pour beaten egg into the middle. Scramble the egg.

Add noodles to the pan and pour sauce over the mixture. Reduce heat to medium-low. The mixture will look saucy at first but let it cook at least 5 minutes, stirring frequently and it will thicken.

Stir in bean sprouts and remove from heat. Top with peanuts and cilantro. Serve with lime wedges.

Serves 4.

Note: I recommend doubling the sauce and refrigerating for leftovers.

Bihon Pancit

Ingredients

1 tablespoon peanut oil

1 boneless, skinless chicken breast, cooked and diced

2 garlic cloves, minced

1 small onion, finely chopped

1 8 oz package rice noodles

1 1/2 cups mixed, chopoped vegetables (shredded cabbage, scallions, carrots, etc)

Sauce

2 cups low sodium chicken stock

2 tablespoons Aloha Shoyu soy sauce

2 tablespoons dark soy sauce

1 tablespoon oyster sauce

1 teaspoon sugar

2 tablespoons lemon juice + lemon wedges to serve

salt and pepper to taste

Directions

In a wok or large pan, over medium heat, add oil and chicken. Cook until tender. Transfer to a plate and set aside. Add garlic and onion, cook for 2 minutes. Add cooked chicken and season with salt and pepper. Stir in the vegetables, cook additional 3-4 minutes or until tender.

Whisk sauce ingredients together in a medium sized bowl. Pour into pan with vegetables and turn heat to medium high. Bring to a boil.

Add rice noodles and stir until all the noodles are coated with sauce. Keep stirring and cooking until noodles are tender (about 4-5 minutes). Add more water or chicken stock if the dish is too dry before noodles are tender. Season with more salt and pepper, if necessary. Serve immediately with lemon wedges.

Serves 6.

Chicken Teriyaki

Ingredients

2 lbs boneless, skinless chicken thighs
1 cup soy sauce
1 cup sugar
2 teaspoons ginger paste
1 large garlic clove, minced
3 scallions, diced

Directions

For Teriyaki Sauce: Mix soy sauce and sugar in a small saucepan over medium heat and cook 5-10 minutes or until sugar has dissolved. Add remaining ingredients. Stir well.

For Chicken: With a meat tenderizer, pound chicken to tenderize then place in a large zip lock bag. Pour half of the teriyaki sauce over chicken and massage through the bag. Allow to marinate in the refrigerator at least 24 hours for best flavor. Reserve remaining sauce and refrigerate.

Grill chicken the next day, basting every 5-7 minutes or bake in the oven at 425 degrees and baste every 10 minutes. Serve hot with sticky rice and macaroni salad.

Serves 4.

Mochiko Chicken

Ingredients

5 lbs boneless, skinless chicken thighs, cut into thirds

2/3 cup cornstarch

1/3 cup mochiko flour

1/3 cup sugar

1/3 cup soy sauce

2 tablespoons oyster sauce

1/2 teaspoon sesame oil

1 teaspoon garlic, minced

2 tablespoons green onion, chopped

2 eggs

Oil for frying

1 tablespoon sesame seeds

1 1/2 teaspoons red pepper flakes

Mochiko Sauce

1/3 cup sugar

1/3 cup soy sauce

2 tablespoons oyster sauce

1/2 teaspoon sesame oil

1 teaspoon minced garlic

red pepper flakes to taste

sesame seeds, to serve

Directions

For the chicken: In a large, resealable container, add all ingredients together (except oil for frying). Seal and allow to marinate overnight. This is a must! The flavor is much deeper the next day when you cook it.

Heat oil in a large skillet or deep fat fryer and cook until golden brown. Drain on paper towel lined baking sheet.

For the sauce: combine all ingredients in a medium saucepan over high heat except sesame seeds. Bring to a boil. Reduce heat to simmer for 10 minutes until slightly thickened. Remove from heat. Toss chicken in sauce and top with sesame seeds.

Serve hot with sticky rice and macaroni salad.

Serves 4-6.

HULI HULI CHICKEN

Ingredients
1 3 lb chicken, cut into sections

Sauce
1 cup pineapple juice

1/2 cup soy sauce

1/2 cup ketchup

2 tablespoons red wine vinegar

1/2 cup light brown sugar

2 teaspoons ground ginger or ginger paste

Rub
1 tablespoon garlic powder

2 teaspoons paprika

1 teaspoon onion powder

1 teaspoon ground cumin

1 tablespoon kosher salt

1/2 teaspoon cayenne pepper

1/2 teaspoon black pepper

Directions

Preheat oven to 400 degrees. Line a baking sheet with aluminum foil and coat with cooking spray. Place a wire baking rack on the baking sheet.

In a small saucepan over medium heat, combine all sauce ingredients and bring to a boil. Reduce heat to low and simmer 10 minutes or until mixture has thickened, stirring occasionally. Reserve half of the sauce for serving, the rest will be used for basting.

In a small bowl, combine rub ingredients. Mix well. Coat chicken evenly with spice mixture and place on baking rack. Roast chicken for 1 hour or until no longer pink in the middle, turning over each half every 10 minutes and brushing the sauce on each time. Do not baste chicken the last 10 minutes of cooking.

Serve chicken hot with additional sauce.

Serves 4-6.

Slow Cooker Sticky Ribs

Ingredients

2 racks baby back beef ribs (or pork)

Dry Rub

1/2 cup light brown sugar

1 tablespoon smoked paprika

2 teaspoons chili powder

1 tablespoon garlic powder

1 teaspoon pepper

2 tablespoons kosher salt

Sticky Sauce

2 teaspoons ginger paste

2 teaspoons ground pepper

1 teaspoon onion powder

6 cloves garlic, minced

1 1/2 tablespoons sweet chili sauce

2/3 cup soy sauce

2/3 cup balsamic vinegar

2/3 cup light brown sugar

2/3 cup honey

1 tablespoon cornstarch + 1 tablespoon water

Directions

Mix dry rub ingredients together in a small bowl. Remove membrane from ribs and massage both sides of ribs with the rub. Place in slow cooker curved around the edges or cut up and placed on top of each other.

To make the sticky sauce, whisk together all ingredients except for the cornstarch and water. Pour sauce in a medium sized bowl. Reserve half of the sticky sauce, set aside. Add remaining sauce over the ribs and cook on low heat 6-8 hours, until ribs are tender.

Remove ribs from slow cooker and place them on a foil lined pan, meaty side up. Brush sauce from the slow cooker on top of the ribs and broil on high heat until edges start to look crisp. Remove from oven.

Cook remaining sauce on stove top in a medium sized saucepan on low heat. Add the cornstarch and water plus 1 tablespoon of hot liquid from the slow cooker. Whisk well until mixture starts to thicken. Remove from heat and brush on top of hot ribs.

Serves 6.

Mongolian Beef

Ingredients

2 lbs beef tenderloin or beef chuck, cut into strips

1/2 cup cornstarch

Oil for deep fat frying

For the sauce

1 tablespoon ground ginger or ginger paste

1 tablespoon minced garlic

1/2 cup soy sauce

1/2 cup rice vinegar

1/2 cup water

1 teaspoon hoisin sauce

1/2 cup brown sugar

1 teaspoon cornstarch diluted in 3 teaspoons water

1 1/2 teaspoons dried chili flakes

1/2 cup green onion, diced

Directions

Heat enough oil in a large frying pan or wok on medium heat to coat the bottom of the pan. Toss beef strips in cornstarch. Make sure strips are coated evenly. Deep fry beef for 3-5 minutes. Drain oil and set beef aside on paper towel to drain.

In a small saucepan, heat 1 tablespoon oil on medium high heat. Add in ginger and garlic. Stir quickly for 10-15 seconds. Immediately add in soy sauce, water, rice vinegar and hoisin. Bring sauce to a boil. Add brown sugar and cornstarch mixture. Whisk well. Reduce heat to simmer.

Add beef strips, green onion and pepper flakes. Stir to coat. Serve hot.

Serves 4.

Beef and Broccoli

Ingredients

3 tablespoons cornstarch, divided

1/2 cup water + 2 tablespoons, divided

1 teaspoon garlic powder

1 lb boneless round steak or chuck steak cut into thin 3 inch strips

2 tablespoons vegetable oil, divided

4 cup broccoli florets

1 small onion, chopped

1/3 cup soy sauce

2 tablespoons brown sugar

1 1/2 teaspoons ground ginger or paste

Directions

In a bowl, combine 2 tablespoons cornstarch, 2 tablespoons water and garlic powder until smooth. Add beef and toss until well coated.

In a large skillet or wok, over medium high heat, stir fry beef in 1 tablespoon oil until beef reaches desired doneness. Remove and keep warm.

Stir fry broccoli and onion for 4-5 minutes in same pan. Return beef to pan. Combine soy sauce, brown sugar, ginger and remaining cornstarch and water until smooth and add to the pan. Cook for 5-7 minutes. Serve hot over rice.

Serves 4.

Garlic and Beef Noodle Bowls

Ingredients

2 tablespoons oil

1 lb skirt steak, cut into thin strips

4 cloves garlic, minced

1 1/2 teaspoons ground ginger or paste

1/4 cup soy sauce

2 tablespoons brown sugar

1 teaspoon sesame oil

8 oz udon or lo mein noodles

2 tablespoons sliced green onion

1 tablespoon toasted sesame seeds

Directions

Cook noodles according to package directions, drain and set aside.

In a small bowl, mix together brown sugar, soy sauce and sesame oil. Stir well, set aside.

Heat oil over medium high heat in a large skillet or wok. Once hot, add beef strips and cook 2-3 minutes, just until beef is browned. Add garlic and ginger. Cook for 1 minute or until fragrant.

Add soy sauce mixture to pan. Bring to a simmer and cook for 3-5 minutes or until sauce slightly thickens. Add cooked noodles to pan, stir to coat. Toss with green onion and sesame seeds then serve.

Serves 4.

Korean Burritos

Ingredients

Flank Steak

1 1/2 lbs flank steak or short ribs, bones removed

1/4 cup green onions, finely chopped

1/4 cup Aloha Shoyu soy sauce

2 tablespoons brown sugar

1 tablespoon sugar

1 tablespoon toasted sesame oil

1 tablespoon ginger paste

2 cloves garlic, minced

1 tablespoon red pepper flakes

pinch of black pepper

1 tablespoon rice wine vinegar

1 whole pear, peeled and cored

Spicy Sauce

4 tablespoons gochujang paste (Korean chili paste)
1 tablespoon toasted sesame oil
2 tablespoons brown sugar
1 tablespoon soy sauce
1 tablespoon water
3 teaspoons rice vinegar
3 teaspoons minced garlic
1 tablespoon toasted sesame seeds

Burritos

Extra large flour tortillas
Sticky rice
Pickled vegetables
1/2 cup chopped cilantro
shredded lettuce (optional)

Directions

Steak or Ribs:

Combine all ingredients for the sauce in a blender and puree until smooth.

Place steak in a resealable container or plastic bag and pour the marinade over. Refrigerate overnight or a minimum of 6 hours.

Grill the next day until desired temperature is reached or you may cook on low heat in the slow cooker, adding all the marinade to tenderize beef for 8-10 hours.

Sauce:

Combine all ingredients in a small bowl, whisk well. Set aside.

Using a large tortilla, place about 1/2 cup of sticky rice then top with a thin layer of steak. Spoon pickled vegetables on top, then cilantro, lettuce (if desired) and spicy sauce. Roll tightly. Cut in half and serve.

Serves 6.

Bibimbap

Ingredients

1 lb thinly sliced rib eye, sirloin or skirt steak
stir fry oil, for frying all ingredients as you go
4 garlic cloves, minced
2 cups bean sprouts
4 tablespoons soy sauce, divided
2 tablespoons sesame oil, divided
1 cup julienned carrots
12 oz fresh spinach
8 oz fresh shiitake mushrooms, divided
4 eggs
2 tablespoons toasted sesame seeds

Korean Sauce

2 tablespoons gochujang chili paste
1 tablespoon sesame oil
1 teaspoon sugar
1 tablespoon water
1 teaspoon apple cider vinegar
1 teaspoon garlic, minced

Directions

Cook sushi rice. Set aside.

Prepare Bulgogi: Stir fry steak with salt, pepper, 1 tablespoon soy sauce and sesame oil. Set aside.

Cook bean sprouts in boiling water for 5 minutes. Drain, place in a separate bowl and add 1 teaspoon garlic and 1 tablespoon each of soy sauce and sesame oil. Whisk together, set aside.

Stir fry the carrots in 1 tablespoon oil for 4 minutes. Lightly salt.

Stir fry spinach with a teaspoon of water until wilted and water has evaporated, about 4 minutes. Place in a separate bowl, add 1 teaspoon minced garlic, 1 tablespoon soy sauce and sesame oil. Set aside.

Stir fry mushrooms with 1 tablespoon of soy sauce until reduced and light brown, about 8-10 minutes. Cook 4 eggs, sunny side up, season lightly with salt and pepper, set aside.

Place all sauce ingredients together in a blender and puree until smooth. Pour into a small bowl to serve.

Assemble the dish. Portion out rice into 4 bowls, arrange toppings in a circular fashion. Top each with an egg and sprinkle with sesame seeds. Garnish with sauce.

Serves 4.

Thai Beef Jerky

Ingredients

4 cloves garlic, minced
2 tablespoons toasted sesame seeds
1 teaspoon mushroom powder
1/2 cup pineapple juice
2 tablespoons sriracha sauce
1 tablespoon soy sauce
2 tablespoons dried cilantro
1 1/2 teaspoons lime juice
1 teaspoon dried Thai basil
1 teaspoon red chili flakes

Directions

Trim all the fat off the beef and place in the freezer on a parchment-lined baking tray for at least 2 hours to partially freeze.

Combine garlic, toasted sesame seeds and mushroom powder in a blender to make a paste. Add remaining ingredients and blend well.

Remove the steak from the freezer and cut into thin 1/4 inch strips. Place beef and marinade in a large zip lock bag and marinate overnight (for best results). After the marinating process is over, remove meat from the marinade and pat dry the strips of beef. Dry in your dehydrator or bake in the oven on a parchment lined baking sheet at 175 degrees for 3-4 hours. After 3 hours check the texture, if it needs to dry out more, allow to cook another hour.

The jerky is finished when it bends and cracks, but does not break in half easily.

Serves 6.

Steak Skewers with Korean BBQ Sauce

Ingredients

2 tablespoons canola oil
1/2 cup soy sauce
4 tablespoons lime juice
4 garlic cloves, minced
1 teaspoon ground black pepper
2 lbs flank steak
wooden skewers, soaked in water for 24 hours
sesame seeds and chopped chives, to serve

BBQ sauce

1/2 cup soy sauce
2/3 cup brown sugar
4 garlic cloves, minced
1 1/2 tablespoons rice wine vinegar
1 1/2 tablespoons sweet chili sauce
1 tablespoon ginger paste
1 teaspoon ground black pepper
1 tablespoon cornstarch
1 tablespoon cold water

Directions

In a small bowl, stir together oil, soy sauce, lemon juice, garlic and pepper.
Slice steak thinly across the grain. Combine strips and marinade in a large Ziploc bag and refrigerate overnight.

To make sauce, bring soy sauce, brown sugar, garlic, vinegar, chili sauce, ginger and black pepper to a boil in a small saucepan.

In a small bowl, stir together water and cornstarch. Add to saucepan and simmer sauce until thickened, about 2 to 3 minutes. Thread steak onto skewers. Grill over high heat for 3 minutes. Flip over and grill 1 to 2 more minutes. Serve with green onions, sesame seeds and sauce.

Serves 6.

Black Pepper Beef

Ingredients

1 lb beef steak, cut into small strips

Marinade

1 1/2 tablespoons oyster sauce
1/2 tablespoon light soy sauce
1/4 teaspoon ground pepper
1/4 teaspoon sugar
1/2 tablespoon Chinese cooking wine
2 teaspoons cornstarch
1 teaspoon sesame oil

Stir Fry

cooking oil, as needed
2 garlic cloves, minced
2 fresh green peppers, diced
1/4 red onion, minced
1/2 teaspoon freshly ground black pepper

Directions

Cut beef steak into 1/2 inch wide strips.

Whisk together marinade ingredients in a medium size bowl. Pour over steak in a large Ziplock bag. Marinate overnight.

Add enough oil to cover the bottom of a large frying pan. Add beef strips. Stir fry 3-5 minutes or until steak is lightly browned.

Remove beef, leaving 1 tablespoon of oil in the pan. Fry garlic until aromatic. Fry green peppers and red onion until slightly soft, about 5 minutes. Add a small pinch of salt. Add beef strips and mix well. Add freshly ground black pepper.

Serve hot with noodles or steamed rice.

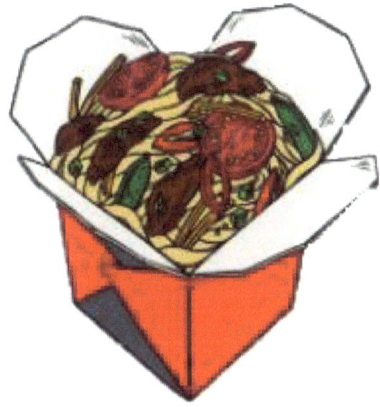

Crock Pot Korean BBQ Tacos with Asian Slaw

Ingredients

Meat

2 lbs pork shoulder
1/2 cup soy sauce
1/2 cup beef stock
1 teaspoon sesame oil
2 tablespoons rice wine vinegar
6 cloves garlic, minced
1 onion, peeled and quartered
1/2 cup brown sugar
1 teaspoon cayenne pepper
salt and pepper to taste

Slaw

1 bag coleslaw mix
1/2 cup white vinegar
1/4 cup sugar
1 teaspoon salt

Tacos

Sliced cucumber
Sliced jalapenos
Fresh cilantro
Soft corn tortillas

Directions

Add all the meat ingredients to the slow cooker. Cook on low for 8 hours or on high for 4 hours. Shred meat and return to crock pot. Leave on warm setting until ready to serve.

Make the slaw: in a large bowl, add vinegar, sugar and salt. Add coleslaw mix and toss to coat. Cover and refrigerate at least one hour.

Assemble Tacos: heat tortillas on the stove or grill and top with a generous portion of meat. Add coleslaw on top and sliced cucumber, jalapeno and cilantro.

Serves 6.

Hawaiian Kalua Pork

Ingredients

1 tablespoon cooking oil
2 lbs pork roast
1 cup water
4 tablespoons liquid smoke
4 tablespoons soy sauce
4 tablespoons brown sugar
1 tablespoon Hawaiian pink salt

Directions

Sear meat on medium high heat on stove top In a dutch oven or cast iron skillet until all sides are browned, about 3-4 minutes per side.

In the slow cooker, add water, liquid smoke, soy sauce, brown sugar and salt. Stir to combine. Place browned pork in slow cooker and cook on low 8-10 hours until tender.

Shred pork in juices and remove with a slotted spoon to serve with white rice and macaroni salad.

Serves 6.

Tonkatsu

Ingredients

4 lbs boneless pork chops, pounded to 1/2 inch thickness
2 eggs, beaten
3/4 cup cornstarch
1 cup water
1 teaspoon garlic salt
1/2 teaspoon black pepper
2 cups panko
Oil for frying

Directions

Heat 1- 1 1/2 inches oil in a large wok or skillet.

Whisk together eggs, cornstarch, water, garlic salt and pepperin a medium size shallow dish to make a thick batter. Dip pork into batter then roll into panko and fry until golden brown on both sides, about 4-5 minutes each side.

Serve hot with katsu sauce, rice and macaroni salad.

Serves 4.

Tonkatsu Sauce

Ingredients

1/4 cup worcestershire sauce
1/2 cup ketchup
1/2 cup sugar
1 cup water
1/2 chicken boullion cube
1/4 teaspoon salt
1/2 teaspoon black pepper
1/2 teaspoon garlic powder
2 teaspoons sriracha sauce
1 tablespoon cornstarch mixed with 1/4 cup water for slurry

Directions

Add all sauce ingredients together, except the slurry mixture. Whisk well then bring to a boil on medium high heat. Add slurry and reduce heat to low, whisk until well combined and sauce has thickened.

Allow sauce to cool completely before serving. Refrigerate leftovers.

Pork Noodle Salad

Ingredients

1 lb pork tenderloin
3 tablespoons sugar
1 tablespoon fish sauce
3 tablespoons sesame oil, divided
1 tablespoon soy sauce
2 teaspoons ground black pepper
1 teaspoon kosher salt
1 large clove garlic, minced

Sauce

1 1/2 cups water
1/4 cup rice vinegar
1 1/2 tablespoons fish sauce
3 tablespoons sugar
1 medium garlic clove, minced
1/2 teaspoon kosher salt
1 pinch korean chili flakes

Salad

12 oz. thin, white rice noodles
4 to 6 cups sliced romaine or iceberg lettuce
1 to 2 large carrots, julienned
half of a large English cucumber, sliced into thin rounds
1 cup bean sprouts
1 bunch fresh cilantro (coarsely chop or tear, if desired)
1 bunch fresh mint (coarsely chop or tear, if desired)
fresh lime wedges

Directions

Pork: Place pork tenderloin in freezer to chill for 30 minutes. Remove from freezer and cut crosswise into very thin slices, about 1/8 inch thick. Cut each slice in half lengthwise. Place pork pieces in a wide, shallow bowl or large Ziploc bag.

In a small bowl, stir together sugar, fish sauce, 1 tablespoon of sesame oil, soy sauce, black pepper, salt and garlic. Pour mixture over pork pieces and fold several times to ensure the marinade is thoroughly mixed in with the pork. Cover bowl and place in refrigerator to marinate for 1 hour. Meanwhile, prepare the sauce and noodles.

Sauce: In a small saucepan over medium to medium-high heat, stir together all sauce ingredients. Once sugar and salt have dissolved, remove from heat to cool to room temperature.

Noodle salad: Bring a large saucepan of water to a boil. Add rice noodles, stir, then turn off heat. Let noodles soften according to the package directions, drain and rinse in cold water in a colander. Shake well to remove water and let set in a colander at room temperature.

Divide noodles among four wide bowls or plates. Top each with lettuce, carrots, cucumber, bean sprouts, cilantro, mint and lime.

Remove pork from refrigerator. Heat a large cast iron skillet over medium-high to high heat. When hot, add remaining 2 tablespoons of the sesame oil and swirl around the bottom of the skillet. When oil is shimmering, carefully add pork. Separate pork pieces to cover bottom of skillet. Let pork sit without stirring for about 1 minute to caramelize. Fold and repeat until pork is cooked through, about 5 minutes. Total cook time will depend on how thin the pork is cut.

Divide hot pork among each of the four bowls. Serve with sauce.

Serves 4.

Spicy Pork Noodles

Ingredients

2 lbs pork loin, thinly cut
10 oz rice noodles
grated carrot, chopped scallions, crushed peanuts and cilantro to top

sauce/marinade

3/4 cup soy sauce
1/2 cup water
1/3 cup sesame oil
1/4 cup honey
1 tablespoon fish sauce
1/3 cup vinegar
2 tablespoons lime juice
3 tablespoons ginger paste
1 large jalapeno pepper
1/4 cup + 2 tablespoons hoisin sauce
1/4 cup creamy peanut butter

Directions

Place all sauce/marinade ingredients in a blender or food processor and blend until smooth. Pour half of the marinade on top of the pork and marinate overnight. Reserve remaining marinade and place in a sealed container, refrigerate.

Heat a nonstick skillet or stove top grill and cook pork until browned on the outside. Set aside.

Cook noodles according to package directions, drain and set aside.

In a large pot, add noodles, extra sauce and pork. Cook on medium low heat for 7-10 minutes until sauce is warm and noodles are well coated. Chop pork into bite size pieces and toss in with warm noodles along with carrots, cilantro, scallions and peanuts. Toss well to combine and serve hot.

Serves 6.

Korean BBQ Pork Ribs

Ingredients

2 lbs short ribs (or if not available, use a lean, boneless pork rib)

For the marinade

1/2 cup soy sauce
4 tablespoons dark brown sugar
2 tablespoons rice wine vinegar
2 tablespoons grated apple or nashi pear
2 tablespoons grated white onion
2 tablespoons minced garlic
1 teaspoon ginger paste
1/2 teaspoon black pepper

Directions

Add all marinade ingredients into a blender and puree until smooth. Set aside.

Rinse and pat dry meat with paper towels. Place meat in a large zip lock bag and add marinade. Refrigerate overnight for best flavor, or 5 hours minimum.

Remove meat and let rest for 30-45 minutes before cooking. Heat grill and spray generously with nonstick cooking spray. Grill ribs until cooked all the way through, brushing with marinade every 5-7 minutes for extra flavor. Serve hot with rice.

Serves 4.

Easy Pork Ramen

Ingredients

2 packages Sapporo Ichiban, (Chicken Flavored) Instant noodles
1 teaspoon korean chili flakes
2 tablespoons minced garlic
1 tablespoon ginger paste
1 teaspoon sesame oil
1 1/2 cups leftover Korean Ribs (page 100), chopped
2 large eggs
2 cups frozen stir fry vegetables

To Serve

2 tablespoons Sambal Oelek garlic sauce
fresh chives

Directions

Heat a large dutch oven on high heat with 2 cups water. Bring to a boil. Add packaged seasoning mix that comes with ramen noodles. Whisk well. Add cooked ribs and cover. Lower heat to medium and allow to simmer.

Heat a small frying pan with sesame oil on low heat. Add garlic and ginger paste. Cook on low for 5-7 minutes or until fragrant. Add to the dutch oven along with korean chili flakes and pepper. Stir in noodles. Simmer 10 minutes. Turn off the heat and remove lid.

Place eggs in a medium saucepan with enough water to cover eggs. Bring to a boil then turn off the heat and cover. Cook for 6 minutes. Remove eggs from water and place in an ice bath to cool. Peel shells off both eggs and slice in half, set aside.

To serve: Ladle even amounts of ramen in two large bowls. Top with fresh chives, two slices of egg and 1 tablespoon Sambal Oelek.

Serves 2.

Spicy Pork Ramen

Ingredients

2 tablespoons olive oil
2 lbs pork shoulder
¼ teaspoon salt
¼ teaspoon pepper
2 carrots, peeled. One left whole, the other cut into matchsticks
1 onion, cut in half
1 stick of celery, broken in half
3 cloves garlic, chopped in half
1 inch piece of ginger, roughly chopped
2 liters (8 1/2 cups) chicken or vegetable stock
2 tablespoons Mirin cooking wine
3 tablespoons soy sauce
2 tablespoons Gochujang Paste
1 red chili, roughly sliced
4 large eggs
8 oz dried ramen noodles
1 leek, sliced
3 cups baby spinach leaves
1 teaspoon toasted sesame seeds
small bunch spring onions scallions, chopped
1 teaspoon Korean chili flakes

Directions

Preheat oven to 300 degrees. Heat a dutch oven on the stove top with 1 tablespoon oil on medium high heat.

Season pork with salt and pepper and sear on all sides on high heat. Remove the pork and turn down the heat to medium. Add in onion, whole carrot, celery, garlic, and ginger. Fry for 5 minutes or until onion starts to soften.

Add stock, Mirin, soy sauce, gochujan, red chili and seared pork. Bring to a boil. Place lid on the dutch oven and cook in the preheated oven for 4 hours.

Check every 30-40 minutes, to see if during cooking you will need to add more boiling water. Top with more boiling water as needed.

Take the dutch oven out after 4 hours, lay the pork on the cutting board and remove any fat. Shred the pork using two forks. Strain the liquid from the pot and discard the vegetables. Place liquid back in the pot with pork and return to stove top and cook on low heat.

Place eggs in a small pan and cover with cold water. Bring to a boil and simmer 6 minutes. Remove from heat and place in a bowl of cold water to stop the cooking process.

Add noodles to a medium pot of boiling water and cook for 5 minutes. Drain and run under cold water (to stop them from sticking.)

Heat the remaining oil in a frying pan. Add leek, salt and pepper and fry for 5 minutes, stirring occasionally. Remove the leek from the pan and allow to wilt for 1 minute.

Divide the noodles between four bowls. Top with hot broth, shredded pork, leek, spinach and carrot matchsticks.

Peel the eggs and slice in half. Place 2 halves in each bowl. Garnish soup bowls with sesame seeds, spring onions and chili flakes before serving.

Serves 4.

Slow Cooker Moo Shu Pork

Ingredients

2 cups plum sauce

1/4 teaspoon sesame oil

1 tablespoon soy sauce

3 large cloves garlic, minced

1 tablespoon cornstarch

1 bag (16 ounces) shredded coleslaw mix

1/2 bag (10 ounces) shredded carrots

3/4 pound boneless pork loin chops

12 large wonton wrappers

scallion strips (optional)

3-4 tablespoons canola oil for wonton wrappers

Directions

Stir together plum sauce, garlic, sesame oil, soy sauce and cornstarch, set aside.

Place coleslaw mix and carrots into slow cooker. Cut the pork into 1/8-inch thick slices, then cut each slice in half lengthwise and sprinkle on top of cabbage mixture in slow cooker. Drizzle with 1/4 cup sauce. Cover and cook on high for 4 hours or low for 6 hours.

Remove cover. Stir in remaining 1/2 cup plum sauce mixture.

Steaming the wrappers

Take one wrapper and brush lightly with oil. Repeat process until you have 20 stacked on top of each other.

Slightly press down on the stack. Using a rolling pin, roll out the stack until they are 4 inches in diameter. Place the wrappers in your steamer and steam 20 minutes. Tear each one off individually as soon as they are done, (you want to do this while they are still warm).

Fold neatly and serve on a platter or serve already stuffed with mixture: Place 1/2 cup pork mixture in center of each "wrap", top with scallion strips and roll up. Serve warm.

Serves 4-6.

Pork Banh Mi Sandwiches

Ingredients

1 lb roasted and chilled pork belly

Pickled Vegetables

1/3 cup rice wine vinegar

1 cup warm water

4 tablespoons sugar

1 tablespoon sea salt

2 carrots, peeled

1/2 large Daikon radish, peeled

1 jalapeno pepper, seeded and sliced

Pork

1 tablespoon canola oil

2 cloves garlic, peeled and minced

1 teaspoon fish sauce

1/2 teaspoon tamarind paste

1 small Thai chile, seeded and thinly sliced

1/2 teaspoon black pepper

1/4 cup sugar

1 tablespoon freshly squeezed lime juice

Sandwiches

2-3 individually sized baguettes

1 cucumber, peeled and thinly sliced

1/2 cup fresh cilantro leaves

Spicy Spread

2 tablespoons mayonnaise

1 teaspoon sriracha sauce

Directions

To make the pickled vegetables, combine rice wine vinegar, warm water, 4 tablespoons sugar and kosher salt in a large bowl and stir to combine until sugar has dissolved.

Use a julienne peeler to grate the carrots and daikon into thin strips. Place the carrot and daikon into the pickle brine. Add sliced jalapeno. Cover and refrigerate vegetables for at least 8 hours .

To make the pork belly, cut the roasted and chilled pork belly into 1 inch cubes and set aside. Heat canola oil in a saucepan over medium heat, add garlic and saute until fragrant, about 60 seconds. Add fish sauce, tamarind paste, Thai chile and peppercorns, cook for 1 minute. Add pork belly to the mixture.

Stir the pork belly to coat with sauce and cook until it begins to brown on the edges, about 10-15 minutes. Remove from heat.

In a nonstick frying pan, spread 1/4 cup sugar out in a single layer. Heat the sugar over medium-low heat, keeping a close eye on it but not stirring it. Once all of the sugar has melted, add the pork belly and sauce. Quickly stir to coat with caramelized sugar, then add the lime juice. Cook until pork is fully coated and caramel sauce is thick, about 2-3 minutes, remove from heat and set aside.

To prepare the sandwiches, slice each baguette in half lengthwise. Mix mayonnaise and sriracha together in a small bowl and spread on the bottom half of each baguette.

Place a layer of sliced cucumbers on top of the mayonnaise, then top with pork belly. Place a few large spoonfuls of the pickled carrot and daikon on top of the pork belly, then top that with the cilantro leaves. Close the sandwiches and serve immediately.

Serves 4.

Crab Casserole

Ingredients

16 oz fresh crab
1/2 cup sour cream
1 tablespoon lemon juice
1/4 teaspoon garlic salt
1 1/4 cups shredded cheddar cheese, divided
8 oz cream cheese, softened
2 tablespoons mayonnaise
1 1/4 teaspoons Worcestershire Sauce
1 tablespoon sugar
1 tablespoon milk

Directions

Reserve half of the cheddar cheese to sprinkle on top of the casserole. Add remaining ingredients into a large bowl, stirring well to combine.

Preheat oven to 350 degrees. Spray a large casserole dish with nonstick cooking spray.

Spoon crab mixture into baking dish and sprinkle remaining cheese on top. Bake for 30 minutes or until cheese is bubbly and lightly browned on top.

Serves 4-6

Happy Family

Ingredients

Stir Fry

1 large boneless, skinless chicken breast
1/2 lb flank steak
1 tablespoon baking soda
1 cup broccoli florets
1/4 cup carrots, shredded
1 can baby corn, drained and cut into bite size pieces
1 1/2 tablespoons oil
1/4 teaspoon salt
12 large raw shrimp
1/2 cup mushrooms, sliced
1/2 cup water chestnut slices
3 green onions, sliced
4 garlic cloves, minced

For the Sauce

3/4 cup chicken broth
2 tablespoons cornstarch
3 tablespoons Chinese cooking wine
2 tablespoons oyster sauce
2 tablespoons soy sauce
1 teaspoon red pepper flakes
1 teaspoon black pepper
1 teaspoon brown sugar

Directions

Slice beef across the grain into 1/4 inch thick strips and put aside in a medium sized bowl. Slice chicken across the grain into 1/4 inch thick strips and place in separate medium sized bowl.

Sprinkle half a tablespoon of baking soda over the beef and half a tablespoon of baking soda over the chicken. Gently turn the meat until lightly coated. Set meat mixture aside for 15 minutes.

Rinse both meats well and pat dry with paper towels.

Place a large nonstick skillet over medium high heat and cook vegetables 5-7 minutes with 1/4 cup water until tender, set aside.

Mix cornstarch and chicken broth together, then add the Chinese cooking wine, oyster sauce, soy sauce, garlic, salt, pepper and brown sugar. Stir well. Add to a large pot and bring to a low boil. Turn heat down to low and simmer 5-7 minutes.

Place a large skillet on medium high heat with 1 tablespoon vegetable oil. Cook chicken and beef about 2-3 minutes on each side. Add shrimp, cook just one minute on each side, do not overcook! Add meat and vegetables to the large pot, stirring well to coat. Cover with lid and allow to simmer additional 5 minutes. Serve hot with rice.

Serves 4

Coconut Shrimp

Ingredients

1 lb medium shrimp, fresh or frozen (thawed)
1/3 cup cornstarch
1 teaspoon salt
1 teaspoon black pepper
vegetable oil for frying
1/2 cup coconut milk
1/4 cup sweetened condensed milk
3 tablespoons mayonnaise

Directions

Heat oil to 350 degrees in a skillet or pan. Add cornstarch, salt and pepper in a Ziploc bag. Add shrimp to cornstarch mixture and shake until fully coated. Remove shrimp from bag and fry until light golden brown (between 3-5 minutes depending on size of shrimp). Drain on a paper towel until ready to use.

Combine mayonnaise, coconut milk and condensed milk in a saucepan over medium high heat. Heat until it comes to a boil, stirring to prevent burning, cooking about 5 minutes.

Toss shrimp into coconut mixture and bring just to a boil. Remove from heat.
Serve over rice.

Serves 2

Chinese Pepper Shrimp

Ingredients

1 jalapeno pepper
2 cloves garlic, sliced
2 spring onions (just the green tops)
1 lb medium sized shrimp (if using frozen shrimp, thaw in a bowl of cold water)
potato starch (or flour)
salt and pepper
vegetable oil for frying

Directions

Slice jalapeno into rings. Peel and slice garlic. Cut spring onions into long thin rectangles; about 2-3 inches long.

Salt the shrimp and sprinkle with potato starch (or flour). Heat about an inch of oil in a small pot. Oil is hot if you sprinkle water in and the water droplets sizzle. Deep fry shrimp until it turns bright red/orange. Remove the shrimp from hot oil, sprinkle with salt and pepper.

In a frying pan, heat oil and stir fry the deep-fried shrimp along with the hot peppers, garlic and green onions.

Serves 4

Singapore Noodles

Ingredients

Sauce

2 tablespoons soy sauce
2 tablespoons Chinese cooking wine
3 teaspoons curry powder
1/2 teaspoon sugar
1 teaspoon black pepper

Stir Fry

3 oz dried vermicelli noodles
2 tablespoons vegetable oil, separated
10 medium sized raw shrimp, peeled & deveined
2 eggs, beaten
1 small white onion, thinly sliced
4 garlic cloves, minced
1 teaspoon ginger paste
1/2 lb prepared chinese bbq pork, diced
1 cup diced red bell pepper
1 small jalapeno pepper, diced

Directions

Combine sauce ingredients in a small bowl, set aside.

Cook noodles according to package instructions. Drain and set aside.

Heat 1 tablespoon of oil in a large wok or frying pan on medium high heat. Cook shrimp about a minute on each side, remove from pan and drain on a paper towel lined pan or plate.

Add egg and whisk, making eggs light and fluffy. Remove eggs from wok and set aside.

Add remaining 1 tablespoon of oil to the wok or pan and cook ginger, garlic and onion for 5-7 minutes; reducing heat to low. Cook until garlic is fragrant and onion is slightly softened. Add bell pepper and jalapeno and cook an additional minute.

Add noodles and sauce to the pan. Stir in eggs and shrimp. Toss to combine and cook additional 5 minutes until heated through. Serve hot.

Serves 4

Spicy Fried Shrimp

Ingredients

Sauce

1/2 cup mayonnaise
4 teaspoons sweet chili sauce
1 teaspoon honey
1/2 teaspoon rice vinegar

Shrimp

3/4 cup buttermilk
1 egg
1 cup panko
1 cup flour
1 teaspoon ground sage
1 teaspoon black pepper
1/2 teaspoon onion powder
1/2 teaspoon garlic powder
1/2 teaspoon dried basil
1/2 teaspoon Korean chili flakes
20 large raw shrimp, peeled & deveined
canola oil for frying
Optional: 2 tablespoons chives to serve

Directions

Combine all sauce ingredients in a medium size bowl, whisking well to combine. Refrigerate until ready to use.

Whisk buttermilk and egg in a large bowl until well mixed. Combine the remaining ingredients in a large mixing bowl, set aside. Dip each shrimp in buttermilk mixture then in flour mixture. Place breaded shrimp on a large baking sheet and refrigerate 1 hour.

Heat oil to 350 degrees in a large wok or deep skillet. Cook 4-6 shrimp at a time, 2-3 minutes on each side and drain on paper towel lined plate or baking sheet.

Toss shrimp in spicy sauce and garnish with chives, if desired.

Serves 4

Sushi Bowls

Ingredients

2 cups sticky rice
2 tablespoons seasoned rice vinegar
2 tablespoons sugar
1 teaspoon salt
2 large ripe avocados, sliced
2 medium sized cucumbers, sliced thin
12 oz fresh crab (or krab sticks, cooked shrimp, smoked salmon, tempura shrimp, poke, etc.)
1/2 tablespoon toasted sesame seeds

Sauce

1/3 cup Kewpie (Japanese) mayonnaise
1 teaspoon sriracha sauce
1 teaspoon toasted sesame oil
1 teaspoon rice vinegar

Directions

Prepare rice according to directions. Combine seasoned rice vinegar with salt and sugar in a small dish. Microwave 30 seconds-1 minute or until sugar dissolves. Stir well. Toss with sticky rice until well coated.

Divide sticky rice among 4 bowls. Top with avocado, cucumber and crab (or your choice of fish).

For the sauce, whisk all ingredients in a medium size bowl and refrigerate overnight or for at least 1 hour. Drizzle over prepared bowls.

Serves 4

Poached Salmon with Coconut Curry Sauce

Ingredients

4 salmon fillets
salt and pepper
2 tablespoons oil
2 garlic cloves, minced
2 teaspoons ginger paste
1 tablespoon lemongrass paste
1 tablespoon brown sugar
1 teaspoon Sambal Oelek chili sauce
14 oz coconut milk
1 tablespoon soy sauce
2 teaspoons lime zest
Lime juice, *to taste*

Garnish

Fresh cilantro, *finely chopped*
Finely sliced large red chillies *(optional)*
Vermicelli noodles, *or rice*
Steamed Asian greens

Directions

Season both sides of salmon with salt and pepper. Heat 1 tablespoon oil in a nonstick pan or well seasoned skillet over medium high heat. Add salmon and sear for 2 minutes, or until golden brown. Remove and place on a plate.

Turn heat to medium low. Heat remaining oil and add garlic, ginger and lemongrass. Cook garlic until light golden and fragrant, about 1-2 minutes. Add sugar and cook for 20-30 seconds or until it becomes a caramel color. Stir in chili sauce. Whisk in coconut milk and stir, scraping the bottom to dissolve any bits stuck to the base of the sauce. Add soy sauce and increase heat to medium, simmer 3-5 minutes. Add salmon and simmer gently for an additional 4-5 minutes or until cooked all the way through. Remove salmon, stir in lime zest and juice to taste. Serve salmon over rice or noodles.

Serves 2.

Traditional Chow Mein

Ingredients

1/4 cup soy sauce

4 cloves garlic, minced

1 1/2 tablespoons brown sugar, packed

2 teaspoons grated ginger or ginger paste

1 teaspoon black pepper

2 5 oz packages Yaki-Soba noodles

1 large white onion, diced

3 stalks celery, sliced diagonally

2 cups shredded cabbage

2 tablespoons oil

Directions

In a small bowl, whisk together soy sauce, garlic, ginger, brown sugar and pepper. Set aside.

In a large pot of boiling water, cook Yaki-Soba noodles for 2 minutes. Drain well, set aside.

Heat a large wok or frying pan on medium heat and add oil. Cook celery and onion 3-5 minutes or until onion is translucent. Stir in cabbage until heated through, 2-3 minutes. Stir in noodles and sauce mixture until well combined, about 3-5 minutes. Serve hot.

Fried Rice

Ingredients

4 cups leftover, cooked white rice
4 eggs, beaten
4 tablespoons butter, divided
3/4 cup frozen peas and carrots
1/2 cup diced white onion
3 tablespoons soy sauce
1 teaspoon sesame oil
1 teaspoon ground black pepper
1/2 teaspoon salt
1/2 cup green onion, diced (including green tops)

Directions

Scramble eggs in a large skillet over medium heat with 2 tablespoons of butter. After eggs are cooked, chop the scrambled eggs into pea size amounts with spatula. Stir into the bowl of cooked rice along with thawed peas, carrots and onion. Stir until well combined.

Melt remaining butter in a large wok or skillet on medium high heat. When the butter has melted, add rice mixture and stir for 5 minutes. While rice is cooking, mix the soy sauce and sesame oil together in a small dish. Pour evenly over the rice and stir to coat well. Saute about 10 minutes, stirring and turning frequently until rice mixture is browned. Add salt and pepper to taste. Top with green onion.

Serves 4.

Macaroni Salad

Ingredients

1 lb box macaroni noodles
2 tablespoons apple cider vinegar
2 large carrots, shredded
1/4 cup sweet onion, shredded
2 1/2 cups Best Foods Mayonnaise (or Hellman's)
1/4 cup milk
2 teaspoons sugar
salt and pepper to taste

Directions

Cook macaroni noodles in a large pot of boiling water until al dente, do not overcook! Drain.

Add noodles to a large bowl (while they are still hot) and add onion and carrot. Sprinkle vinegar over the top and stir well. Cool.

In a small bowl, add remaining ingredients and whisk together well. Once noodles are completely cooled, add mayonnaise mixture and stir until well combined.

Best if chilled overnight or at least 3 hours before serving.

Serves 6.

Pickled Vegetable Slaw

Ingredients

Brine

1/2 cup rice vinegar
1/2 cup apple cider vinegar
2 tablespoons kosher salt
2 tablespoons honey
1/2 tablespoon Korean chili flakes
1 cup distilled water
4 cups julienned vegetables (a combination of carrot, cucumber, onion, jalapenos and radishes)

Directions

Julienne equal portions of vegetables and distribute into 4 small jars or 1 large glass jar.

To make brine, heat the vinegars, honey, salt and chili flakes in a medium sized pot until mixture comes to a simmer. Remove from heat and whisk in water. Allow brine to cool to room temperature before pouring over jar(s) of julienned vegetables.

Refrigerate for at least 24 hours. Make sure vegetables are submerged completely in the brine mixture for maximum shelf life and flavor.

Traditional Korean Kimchi

Ingredients

1 medium Napa cabbage
4 oz Daikon radish or half of a large radish, julienned
2 radishes for garnish, julienned (optional)
3 oz white onion or 1/4 of a large onion, julienned x2 (half for blending and half for mixing)
1 teaspoon ginger, roughly chopped
6 cloves of garlic, roughly chopped
2 red jalapeno peppers
2 teaspoons red dried chili powder
½ teaspoon sugar or Splenda
1 tablespoon cooked, sweet rice or sweet rice powder
1 tablespoon water for blending
1/2 cup chives
2 tablespoons sea salt, as needed

Directions

To make one 24 oz jar of Kimchi:

Soak cabbage for two hours in 2 tablespoons of salt with one cup of water. Note: the longer you soak the cabbage, the saltier your kimchi will turn out. It's important to not soak for too long!

Rinse off the salt water with fresh cold water.

Stir together 1/2 radish, onion, ginger, garlic, peppers, red chili powder, sugar and sweet rice. (Make sure that the sweet rice is cooked). Combine this mixture with the the cabbage.

Add in the chopped chives as a garnish. To ferment, put the Kimchi in an airtight container and store at room temperature for 24 hours. After 24 hours, the Kimchi can be stored in the refrigerator.

Chinese Cabbage Stir Fry

Ingredients

1 medium size cabbage
2 garlic cloves, sliced
1 tablespoon ginger paste
3-6 dried chili peppers (depending on your preference)
1/2 teaspoon Sichuan peppercorn
1 tablespoon light soy sauce
1/2 tablespoon black vinegar
1/2 teaspoon salt, or as needed
1 tablespoon vegetable cooking oil

Directions

Hand tear the cabbage, keeping the tender green leaves only. Discard the hard white part. Wash gently and drain completely.

Heat wok on medium high heat, add oil. Add dried chili pepper, ginger paste and Sichuan peppercorn. Saute until aromatic. Stir in garlic.

Add cabbage immediately. Quick fry the cabbage, add salt, light soy sauce and vinegar.

Serves 2.

Chinese Buffet-Style Green Beans

Ingredients

1 tablespoon sesame oil
2 large garlic cloves, minced
1 lb fresh green beans, trimmed
1 tablespoon sugar
2 tablespoons oyster sauce
1 teaspoon soy sauce
toasted sesame seeds to top

Directions

In a large wok or frying pan, heat oil on low heat. Add garlic and cook until lightly browned and fragrant. Add sugar, oyster sauce and soy sauce. Whisk to combine. Add green beans and cook until desired tenderness (about 5-7 minutes).

Sprinkle sesame seeds over green beans before serving.

Serves 4.

Chinese Style Mushrooms

Ingredients

16 oz whole mushrooms
1/2 cup cold water (for slurry)
1 tablespoon cornstarch
1 tablespoon canola oil
1/2 cup water (for the sauce)
1/4 cup oyster sauce
1 1/2 tablespoons soy sauce

Directions

Wash mushrooms and drain.

Combine 1/2 cup cold water and cornstarch for slurry; set aside.

Heat oil over medium high heat in a large skillet or wok. When the oil is ready (a drop of water will dance in the skillet), add the mushrooms. Stir fry until the desired tenderness is reached or until the water from the mushrooms starts to cook off.

Add 1/2 cup water, oyster sauce and soy sauce to the skillet. Stir well and bring to a boil. Slowly add slurry to the skillet. Stir until the sauce thickens.

Serves 4

Hawaiian Cake Noodle

Noodles:

1 pound fresh Saimin (Hong Kong egg noodles)

4 tablespoons oil

Directions

Place noodles in a large pot of boiling water and cook for 2–3 minutes. Drain noodles into a colander and set aside.

Heat 4 tablespoons of oil in a large nonstick frying pan or wok over medium-high heat. Add the drained noodles and spread evenly to form a noodle cake that covers the bottom of the pan. Cook noodles until crisp and golden brown. Flip the noodle cake over to crisp the other side. More oil may be needed to complete the process.

Remove crisp noodle cake to a cutting board and cut into square portions. Arrange on a serving platter.

Sauce

3 cups chicken stock

3 tablespoons oyster sauce

2 tablespoons soy sauce

2 teaspoons sesame oil

2 teaspoons kosher salt

1 teaspoon sugar

1/2 teaspoon white pepper

Slurry

6 tablespoons cornstarch

1 cup water

Directions

Place chicken stock and seasonings in a medium sauce pot and bring to a boil.

Mix cornstarch and water together and whisk into the boiling stock to thicken.

Place noodle cake in a small bowl and ladle sauce on top to serve.

Serves 8.

INDEX

A

B
BBQ Pork, **13**
Beef and Broccoli, **78**
Bibimbap, **83**
Bihon Pancit, **66**
Black Pepper Beef, **88**
Bourbon Chicken, **42**

C
Caramelized Lemongrass Chicken, **49**
Cashew Chicken, **40**
Chicken Lettuce Wraps, **14**
Chicken Pad Thai, **62**
Chicken Pad Thai 2, **64**
Chicken Teriyaki, **68**
Chinese Buffet-Style Green Beans, **130**
Chinese Cabbage Stir Fry, **129**
Chinese Chicken Batter 1, **31**
Chinese Chicken Batter 2, **32**
Chinese Pepper Shrimp, **115**
Chinese Pork Meatballs, **23**
Chinese Style Mushrooms, **131**
Coconut Shrimp, **114**
Crab Casserole, **111**
Cream Cheese Rangoon, **12**
Crispy Green Beans, **21**
Crock Pot Korean BBQ Tacos with Asian Slaw, **91**

D

E
Easy Pork Ramen, **101**
Easy Sweet and Sour Meatballs, **25**
Egg Rolls, **6**
Evil Jungle Princess (Thai Curry), **60**

F
Fried Rice, **124**

G
Garlic and Beef Noodle Bowls, **80**
General Tso's Sauce, **38**
Grilled Sweet Chili Chicken, **46**

H
Happy Family, **112**
Hawaiian Cake Noodle, **132**
Hawaiian Kalua Pork, **93**
Honey Sesame Sauce, **35**
Honey Sriracha Chicken, **51**
Honey Walnut Sauce, **39**
Huli Huli Chicken, **71**

I

J

K
Korean BBQ Pork Ribs, **100**
Korean Burritos, **81**
Korean Fried Chicken, **52**
Korean Meatballs, **26**

L
Lemon Sauce, **37**
Lumpia, **8**

M
Macaroni Salad, **125**
Mochiko Chicken, **69**
Mongolian Beef, **76**

N

O
Orange Sauce, **33**

P
Peanut Sauce, **19**
Peking Chicken, **47**
Pickled Vegetable Slaw, **126**
Poached Salmon with Coconut Curry Sauce, **121**
Pork Banh Mi Sandwiches, **107**
Pork Noodle Salad, **96**
Pot Stickers, **10**
Pot Sticker Sauce, **11**

Q

R
Rumaki, **28**

S
Salad Rolls, **20**
Singapore Noodles, **116**
Slow Cooker Moo Shu Pork, **105**
Slow Cooker Sticky Ribs, **74**
Spicy Fried Shrimp, **118**
Spicy Pork Noodles, **98**
Spicy Pork Ramen, **103**
Spicy Sauce for Green Beans, **22**
Steak Skewers with Korean BBQ Sauce, **87**
Sushi Bowls, **119**
Sweet and Sour Sauce, **36**
Sweet Chili Dipping Sauce, **19**
Szechuan Chicken, **44**

T
Tamarind Cashew Dipping Sauce, **18**
Thai Beef Jerky, **85**
Thai Chicken Satays, **16**
Thai Coconut Curry Noodles, **17**
Thai Green Curry, **54**
Thai Grilled Chicken, **50**
Thai Lettuce Wraps, **16**
Thai Marinated Cucumbers, **18**
Thai Red Curry, **56**
Thai Yellow Curry, **58**
Tonkatsu, **94**
Tonkatsu Sauce, **95**
Traditional Chow Mein, **123**
Traditional Korean Kimchi, **127**

U

V

W

X

Y

Z

Copyright © 2019 by Sarah Gilbert

All rights reserved. This book or any portion thereof may not be reproduced or used in any manner whatsoever without the express written permission of the publisher except for the use of brief quotations in a book review or scholarly journal.

First Printing: 2019

www.ingramcontent.com/pod-product-compliance
Lightning Source LLC
Chambersburg PA
CBHW041441010526
44118CB00003B/141